FIRST
SPORTS
SOURCE

FIRST SOURCE TO

FOOTBALL

RULES, EQUIPMENT, AND KEY PLAYING TIPS

by Tyler Omoth

AUG 3 1 2016

First
Facts®

CAPSTONE PRESS
a capstone imprint

First Facts are published by Capstone Press,
1710 Roe Crest Drive, North Mankato, Minnesota 56003
www.mycapstone.com

Library of Congress Cataloging-in-Publication Data
Cataloging-in-publication information is on file with the Library of Congress.
ISBN 978-1-4914-8421-0 (library binding)
ISBN 978-1-4914-8430-2 (paperback)
ISBN 978-1-4914-8425-8 (eBook PDF)

Editorial Credits
Mandy Robbins, editor; Heidi Thompson, designer; Eric Gohl, media researcher;
Lori Blackwell, production specialist

Photo Credits
Dreamstime: Americanspirit, cover, Aspenphoto, 20 (top), James Boardman, 21 (top); Newscom:
Cal Sport Media/Duncan Williams, 9, Cal Sport Media/Mike Buscher, 15, Cal Sport Media/Rich
Barnes, 11, Icon SMI/Dustin Bradford, 17, Icon SMI/MSA, 7, Icon Sportswire/Chris Coduto, 19,
Icon Sportswire/Doug Murray, 13, ZUMA Press/Julian H. Gonzalez, 5, ZUMA Press/Trask Smith,
1; Shutterstock: Action Sports Photography, 21 (bottom), Aspen Photo, 20 (bottom)

Design Elements: Shutterstock

Printed and bound in China.
092015   009228S16

TABLE OF CONTENTS

Get In the Game!

Imagine passing footballs like National Football League (NFL) quarterback Aaron Rodgers. Picture yourself catching a **touchdown** pass like star wide receiver Calvin Johnson. Suit up and get in on the action!

TWO WAYS TO PLAY

Full contact football, or *tackle* football, involves tackling the player with the ball. But it can lead to injuries. Tackle football should only be played if you have all the proper gear and padding. Flag football lets players learn the basics of the game without the dangers of tackling. It's a fun option that's safer to play than tackle football.

touchdown—a play in football in which a team carries the ball into the opponent's end zone for six points

tackle—to stop another player by knocking him to the ground

CALVIN JOHNSON

"Football is a game played with arms, legs, and shoulders but mostly from the neck up."

– Knute Rockne, legendary college football coach

CHAPTER 1
Get Ready to Play!

Equipment

Flag football can be played with just the ball and flags attached to each player's hips. Tackle football has a lot more equipment. Players wear helmets to protect their heads. Shoulder, hip, and leg pads make tackling safer. **Cleats** help players run and turn on the grass field without slipping.

FACT
The first football helmets were made of leather. They didn't offer much protection. Today's helmets are made of more advanced materials.

cleats—athletic shoes with spikes on the bottom to help grip dirt and grass playing fields

HELMET

SHOULDER PADS

LEG PADS

CLEATS

The Football Field

Football fields are easy to spot with their green grass and tall **goalposts**. The standard field is 120 yards (110 meters) long and 53 yards (48.5 m) wide. White lines cross the field every 5 yards (4.6 m). On each end there is a 10-yard (9-m) deep end zone with a metal goalpost.

goalpost—a post that marks each end of the field; teams get points for getting the ball through the goalposts

FACT

In the NFL the goalposts were once placed at the front of the end zone. But players often ran into the posts. That led officials to move the goalposts to the back of the end zone in 1974.

CHAPTER 2

How the Game Works

Offense

Eleven players take the field for each team. The offense moves the ball forward to score points. The quarterback leads them. He calls plays and passes the ball. Wide receivers catch passes. Running backs run with the ball. The offensive line blocks defenders from tackling their teammates.

FACT

The NFL championship game is called the Super Bowl. Super Bowl XLIX in 2015 was the most watched TV program in history. It had more than 114 million viewers.

Defense

The defense tries to keep
the offense from scoring.
Defensive linemen tackle
the quarterback and running
backs. Defensive backs tackle
wide receivers. Linebackers patrol
the middle of the field. If the defense
can make an **interception** or **fumble**
recovery, it's called a turnover.

"I like linebackers. I collect
'em. You can't have too
many good ones."
– *Bill Parcells, legendary NFL
head coach.*

interception—a pass caught by a defensive player
fumble—when a player drops the ball or it is
knocked out of his or her hands by another player

Special Teams

Special teams players can have a big impact on a game. Punters **punt** the ball to push the other team back as far as possible. Kickers score points by kicking field goals and extra points. On punts and kickoffs, returners catch the ball and try to score a touchdown. Other special teams players block and tackle.

FACT
The oldest NFL stadium still in use is Chicago's Soldier Field. The first football game held there took place in 1924.

punt—to drop-kick the football to the other team, usually on the 4th down

CHAPTER 3
Rules of the Game

Moving the Ball

When a team is on offense, it gets four **downs**. The offense needs to move the ball 10 yards (9.1 m) or score a touchdown. On the fourth try, the team may choose to punt the ball to its opponents. If the offense is close enough, the **placekicker** can kick a field goal. Successful field goals are worth 3 points.

> **FACT**
>
> Football developed from the sports of soccer and rugby. Born in 1859, Walter Camp is considered the "Father of American Football." He either played, coached, or served on the rules committee for the sport for 25 years.

down—a play in which the offense tries to advance the ball down the field; teams get four downs to go 10 yards

placekicker—a player who attempts to kick a ball through the uprights of a goalpost; a placekicker also does kickoffs

OFFICIALS MEASURE CLOSE CALLS TO SEE IF THE OFFENSE HAS GAINED A FIRST DOWN OR NOT.

Scoring Points

   Getting the ball into the other team's end zone scores a touchdown. A touchdown is worth 6 points. After a touchdown the team can choose to try for an extra point. Extra points are kicked through the goalpost from 33 yards (30 m). Teams can also try for a 2-point conversion by running or passing into the end zone.

ENFORCING THE RULES

Referees watch the action on the field to make sure both teams follow the rules. When someone commits a *penalty*, referees throw yellow flags onto the field. You can recognize referees by their black and white striped uniforms.

penalty—when a player breaks a rule; also refers to a punishment for breaking a rule

CHAPTER 4
Playing Tips

Now that you know the basics of the game, it's time to start practicing! Here are some tips to help you begin.

PASSING

Keep your elbow above your shoulder. Grip the ball with your index finger near the tip of the ball. Step toward your target and snap your wrist downward as you throw the ball. This motion will help you throw a perfect **spiral**.

CATCHING

It's tempting to catch the ball against your chest, but the best receivers use only their hands. Hold your hands close together with your fingers spread out. This method will help you trap the ball and bring it in.

KICKING

Make sure your leg fully completes the kicking motion. Following through on the kick gives greater accuracy and distance. Straight-on kickers use their toes. Soccer-style kickers use the **instep** of the foot.

FACT

Fred Bednarski, a player for the University of Texas, kicked the first soccer-style field goal in 1957.

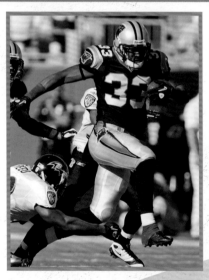

RUNNING

When running with the ball, always keep it tucked tightly into your body. You can hold the ball snugly against your body while leaving the other hand free to block opponents.

spiral—a football thrown with a spin that helps it travel accurately to a receiver

instep—the inside part of your foot between your toes and your ankle

21

Glossary

cleats (KLEETS)—athletic shoes with spikes on the bottom to help grip dirt and grass playing fields

down (DOWN)—a play in which the offense tries to advance the ball down the field; teams get four downs to go 10 yards

fumble (FUHM-buhl)—when a player drops the ball or it is knocked out of his or her hands by another player

goalpost (GOHL-post)—a post that marks each end of the field; players get points for getting the ball through the goalposts

instep (IN-step)—the inside part of your foot between your toes and your ankle

interception (in-tur-SEP-shun)—a pass caught by a defensive player

penalty (PEN-uhl-tee)—a punishment for breaking the rules

placekicker (PLAYSS-kik-ur)—a player who attempts to kick a ball through the uprights of a goalpost; a placekicker also does kickoffs

punt (PUNT)—a play where the ball is dropped and kicked to the other team, usually on 4th down

spiral (SPY-ruhl)—a football thrown with a spin that helps it travel accurately to a receiver

tackle (TACK-uhl)—to stop another player by knocking him to the ground

touchdown (TUCH-down)—a play in football in which a team carries the ball into the opponent's end zone for six points

Read More

Doeden, Matt. *All About Football.* All About Sports. North Mankato, Minn.: Capstone Press, 2015.

Lindeen, Mary. *Let's Play Football!* A Beginning to Read Book. Chicago: Norwood House Press, 2015.

Nagelhout, Ryan. *Football's Greatest Records.* The Greatest Records in Sports. New York: PowerKids Press, 2015.

Internet Sites

FactHound offers a safe, fun way to find Internet sites related to this book. All of the sites on FactHound have been researched by our staff.

Here's all you do:

Visit www.facthound.com

Type in this code: 9781491484210

Check out projects, games and lots more at
www.capstonekids.com

Index